Successful
Cyberm@rketing
in a week

J. JONATHAN GABAY

oughton

HODDER HEADLINE GROUP

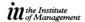

**the Institute
of Management**

The Institute of Management (IM) is the leading
organisation for professional management. Its purpose is
to promote the art and science of management in every
sector and at every level, through research, education,
training and development, and representation of
members' views on management issues.

This series is commissioned by IM Enterprises Limited,
a subsidiary of the Institute of Management, providing
commercial services.

**Management House,
Cottingham Road,
Corby,
Northants NN17 1TT
Tel: 01536 204222;
Fax: 01536 201651
Website: http://www.inst-mgt.org.uk**

Registered in England no 3834492
Registered office: 2 Savoy Court, Strand,
London WC2R 0EZ

Orders: please contact Bookpoint Ltd, 39 Milton Park, Abingdon, Oxon
OX14 4TD.
Telephone: (44) 01235 400414, Fax: (44) 01235 400454. Lines are open from
9.00–6.00, Monday to Saturday, with a 24 hour message answering service.
Email address: orders@bookpoint.co.uk

British Library Cataloguing in Publication Data
A catalogue record for this title is available from The British Library

ISBN 0 340 758155

First published   2000
Impression number   10 9 8 7 6 5 4 3
Year   2004 2003 2002 2001 2000

Typeset by Fakenham Photosettting Limited, Fakenham, Norfolk.
Printed in Great Britain for Hodder & Stoughton Educational, a division of
Hodder Headline Plc, 338 Euston Road, London NW1 3BH by Cox & Wyman
Ltd, Reading, Berkshire.

CONTENTS

For Michelle and Joshua
– with love and admiration

Special thanks to my brother Raphael for being the first to show me the potential of IT and to Gary Brine and Graham Dodridge for stamping the passport to Cyberworld

Tim and Greig for their professionalism, The Institute of Management and Sun Microsystems

F O R E W O R D

Cybermarketing is not an option, it's an imperative. Marketers must learn to play by new rules, blending a mix of traditional skills with the new *dot.com* business model.

The ever flexible Internet adds value to every member of the marketing team. From increasing brand awareness through the creation of a website, on-line demand creation and fulfillment, to introducing new customer loyalty programmes.

As this book practically demonstrates, the web provides the innovation to reach new customers, generate e-mail newsletters, host focus groups, reduce production costs, improve time to market and improve customer tracking and feedback. And much more besides.

The Net economy not only fuels the creative powers of the marketer but provides an information base that allows marketers to make more informed decisions and so have greater impact on business success.

Cybermarketing is a challenge we should all embrace now, from *dot.com*-ing your whole communications strategy to creating an interactive website.

As this book shows, wherever you start, it's never too early to move into cybermarketing and create that competitive edge.

Happy *dot.com*-ing.

Louise Proddow
Head of Marketing Communications and New Media
Sun Microsystems Computers
Louise.Proddow@UK.Sun.com

Technology has always helped markets develop. The railways brought commerce into small communities, the telephone crossed vast plains, the car gave mobility, the computer saved time, and now e-commerce and the custodian of its message – cybermarketing – combines all kinds of communications whilst offering immense market potentials.

Like all industries starting in the kindergarten of enthusiasts and ending as part of the essential rules used in the playground of life, cybermarketing's possibilities are enormous. According to industry experts, we've reached less than ten percent of the Internet's potential marketing value. The extent of the Internet will spread widely at an incredible pace, especially in Europe, where pocket phones – and so access to the Internet via WAP (Wireless Application Protocol) – are particularly popular. By 2008, wireless technology will become second nature to virtually all mobile phone users and even car drivers with in built display modems in their vehicles' dashboards. Not forgetting web links via televisions at home and connections via sophisticated game consoles. Soon, access speeds will reach over two megabytes per second. If the motor industry shared the computer industry's rate of growth since 1990, at today's prices a car would cost no more than £1.93.

So long as there is a demand for products and services, marketing will continue to evolve its methodology according to the available resources that enable organisations like yours meet market needs. Cybermarketing provides today's web-wide marketing solutions for a planet made up of multifarious business communities. Each organisation forming an integral part of those communities needs profitable ways to take advantage of what has become a wired economy.

Today's language of marketing communication relies heavily on the manner in which you disseminate mission-critical information. With the so-called dot.com era, the world is as small as a microchip with marketing opportunities that are equally intricate. The marketing implications of dot.com business solutions are extensive:

- Local values become international issues affecting your marketing plan
- Preparation assumes greater significance
- Your promotions, including direct and awareness marketing, integrate with your total business aspirations
- Campaigns are information-led, driven by customer needs.

Cybermarketed projects get to market faster. Costs to reach your internal as well as external markets are incrementally reduced. Clicks and mortar replace bricks and mortar. In so doing, small business can flourish as well as the bigger players, whilst serving community needs – thus aiding the 'smart growth' economy.

Moreover, despite all its perceived complexity, *dot.com's* business clarity ensures that in practice you no longer have to study to be a computer technologist. Instead, you become a marketing technologist, using a mix of traditional, contemporary and visionary tools.

Over the next seven days you'll learn how to combine your own marketing mix with the dot.com paradigm.

We'll be looking at:

- The evolution of cybermarketing
- How cybermarketing adapts to your audience
- How to promote a cyberbrand
- How to plan a Web-based business
- How to integrate your cyber needs with your customer's desires and suppliers infrastructures
- How to conduct a Web-wide research project
- The secrets behind successful cyber-advertising
- The synergy between traditional marketing and cybermarketing
- How to establish a practical cybermarketing strategy
- Why you should build a cyber portal
- What to look for in a website
- How to chose your ideal ISP
- How to produce creative cyber copy
- How to get your site ranked at the top of a search engine

And much more besides, culminating in my Winning Imperatives of the Web: the essential cybermarketing steps to a profitable Web future.

A wider Web market

The wider Web makes the world a narrower place. Geographic borders are less defined. Deadlines, shorter. International time and distance is as relative as the space between your keyboard and fingertips.

As you read these words, businesses are saving billions of dollars for themselves and their customers through implementing e-commerce sales cycles. For example, vast transportation cost savings are made by comparing logistic tenders by countries on-line.

According to the University of Texas, the Internet is the thirteenth biggest economy in the world. It's no longer just websites, e-commerce, e-solutions or area networks – cybermarketing *is* business and everything attached to it, from mobile phones to music centres. In fact, Web-enabled technology does for your business what Marconi did for keeping the world in touch and Edison for keeping the world informed.

For all this technology, businesses still rely on targeted, value-added sales propositions to draw in new customers whilst securing existing ones. Cybermarketing techniques strengthen relationships with stockholders, employees and suppliers. It touches every aspect of your marketing mix, from sales and distribution to advertising (see Monday). In so doing, cybermarketing positively distinguishes your organisation from that of your competitors. As we progress through this week you will see how.

Explosive e-business

At the time of writing, every four seconds a further eleven organisations establish an Internet presence thereby linking to the world's most successful, broadly spread communications network – the World Wide Web. By 2003, worldwide more than 500 million people will be surfing the Web, from 'Teeny Techies' (aged 6–16) to 'Silver Surfers' (aged 50+).

The popularity of the Internet is only part of a bigger cybermarketing picture. Yet, just taking the Internet, you can measure its incredible growth in a relatively short time scale.

CYBER F@CTS

IT TOOK 38 YEARS FOR RADIO TO ATTRACT 50 MILLION
LISTENERS AND 13 YEARS FOR TELEVISION TO ATTRACT 50
MILLION VIEWERS.

IN JUST 4 YEARS THE INTERNET HAS ATTRACTED 50 MILLION
SURFERS!

Those figures can hardly be balked at, especially when you consider the Internet's beginnings.

From cool to phat

In terms of laying the foundations for cybermarketing the 1950s defined a new generation of teenagers, who became the century's biggest consumers. By 1957, Russia had taken the lead in the space race. So President Eisenhower instructed his defence team to form the Advanced Research Project Agency (ARPA). It comprised both space and nuclear scientists spread widely in several locations. By 1972, a telecommunications computing network connected around 40 research and military establishments. It was called ARPAnet.

The network concept became an electronic data exchange for geeks in universities who experimented with writing lines of computer code. It developed rapidly to become a glamorous electronic bulletin board featuring revealing pictures and has now evolved into the world's fastest, most essential way to conduct business and keep in touch.

From cosmonauts to cybernauts

In the 1970s the world turned 'Big Blue' as IBM put office versions of mainframes on self contained desktop PCs. Technology expanded further with the introduction of lifestyle gadgets like pocket calculators.

Then came the 1980s:

- Courier services 'shrunk' the world
- Fax machines made distances even shorter
- Organisations moved from the stand-alone mainframe and mini-computer/PC towards a networked environment
- Leased line cables from telecommunication companies, (Network Service Providers (NSPs)) connected single site businesses with Local Area Networks
- Wider Area Networks linked offices
- Marketing shifted from mass selling to targeting individuals directly on a data-driven, lump scale.

People were reassured that being an individual with specific goals was okay, providing you connected to something bigger. This was the start of what cybermarketers called the Networked Age.

The 1990s proved to be the vital Web decade. In 1993, the National Centre for Supercomputing Applications (NCSA) developed Mosaic. This enabled surfers to locate information at the click of a mouse.

Thanks to technology and people's largely accepting attitude towards it, power has become more devolved,

CYBER F@CTS

INITIALLY, THE WORLD WIDE WEB WAS TO BE CALLED 'THE INFORMATION MINE' OR 'INFORMATION MESH'. THE TERM 'WORLD WIDE WEB' WAS COINED BY TIM BERNERS-LEE AND ROBERT CAILLIAU. IN 1980, WHILST WORKING AT CERN, THE EUROPEAN LABORATORY FOR PARTICLE PHYSICS NEAR GENEVA, TIM BERNERS-LEE DEVISED A PROGRAM CALLED ENQUIRE. THIS STORED AND RECALLED INFORMATION BASED ON RANDOM ASSOCIATIONS. IN 1989, BERNERS-LEE PROPOSED A WORLD-WIDE SCHEME TO LINK INFORMATION THROUGH A WEB OF HYPERTEXT LINKS. THE FIRST WORLD WIDE WEB PROGRAM DEBUTED ON THE INTERNET IN THE SUMMER OF 1991. THE REST IS HISTORY.

whilst control is better managed. Web technology such as GroupWare frees office staff to share data and entrepreneurs are permitted greater access to international markets.

Less is more

A key business concept during the 90s was 'disintermediation': cutting out middlemen in complex markets. Typically, the scissors were the web and other digital media. As tools, Intranets and Extranets managed corporate internal affairs. Floppy discs went into Zip speed. Tape videos forwarded into video and audio streamed media Web pages. Cumbersome PCs stepped into small footprint workstations. Mini-Discs shrunk into earphone MP3 Players, hand held phones fitted into pocket shirts. TV's turned into digital entertainment centres and diaries became wireless palm held devices, ready to download webpages into the hands of a mobile target audience. The stage was set, the network was switched on: the dot.com CyberAge had arrived.

BUSINESS IS
BOOMING
APPARENTLY

Who is on-line and why?

Today's customers expect businesses to provide goods and services quickly and efficiently and at a location that suits their requirements *more conveniently than yours*. This kind of thinking is a two-way street. Just as your customers and trading partners need to sense that they are in control so you too need to have firm control of your Web business.

The Net-working class

As with traditional marketing, your audience is split into distinctive camps: the internal audience and the external audience.

Both are vital. Your internal audience comprises a community of employees, suppliers, distributors, sales force, consultants, and so on, who typically connect to you via a distributed computing network like a secure Intranet. This internal enterprise-wide network uses the same TCP (Transmission Control Protocol) Internet Protocol technology as the Internet. Using Web browsers, an Intranet network directs information from both the World Wide Web and internal systems to individual company PCs. To prevent unauthorised access by anyone on the World Wide Web, the system is shielded from the outside world by security software called a 'firewall'.

The virtual company bulletin board
In addition to being a tremendous internal communication tool, Intranets can save significant marketing print costs through disseminating anything from a newsletter to internal telephone directory, all of which can be updated regularly.

The external audience

To communicate with external partners like suppliers and sales outlets, you could use an Extranet. This takes a network group of computers beyond the boundaries of an office. It sort of hitches a ride on the back of the World Wide Web using the same electronic dialogue protocols of the Internet. Obviously information is subject to passwords and the network is not open to the general public.

Cyber tip

Check that your site – internal or Internet-wide –
prints. Just because a page is on the screen, it doesn't
mean it will download to an office printer.

Cybercitizens

Your external *Netcitizens* (surfers) are individuals:

- *Prospective buyers* – anyone in the right demographic
  and with appropriate requirements who can be
  encouraged to contact your enterprise.
- *Existing customers* – who have previously dealt with
  you.
- *Borderline customers* – who may leave unless you
  improve your sales support.
- *Lapsing customers* – who want new services.
- *Potential clients* – who, having previously bought
  goods, can be encouraged to buy more.
- *Media* – such as trade and national press journalists
  who want 'real time' access to today's news rather than
  yesterday's headlines.
- *Potential employees* – who want published information.
- *Partners* – teaming up with your organisation and able
  to distribute your products electronically.
- *Would-be investors* – who want solid corporate facts as
  well as reassuring, visionary communications.
- *Allies* – who'll recommend you to others, especially if
  motivated with an incentive.

Which cyber medium suits you?

Cyber benefit	Intranet	Extranet	Cyber vehicle
Strengthen partnerships		√	
Create loyalty programmes		√	www
Build brand awareness			www
Increase business efficiencies	√	√	
On-line company manuals	√		www e-mail Bulletin Board System (BBS)
On-line product demonstrations	√	√	www
On-line departmental conference links via webcams	√	√	www
On-line newsletter	√	√	www e-mail
On-line recruitment	√		www
On-line precision direct marketing	√	√	www
On-line sales training	√	√	
On-line ordering		√	www e-mail Electronic Data Information (EDI)
On-line project tracking	√	√	Agent software EDI
On-line product catalogue		√	www

Cyber benefit	Intranet	Extranet	Cyber vehicle
On-line support	√	√	BBS e-mail www
Mobile/home working computing/ laptop sales links	√		www BBS
Cross-company selling (e.g. Airline ticketing agency linking with a hotel chain)		√	www e-mail
Enhanced customer and employee relationships	√	√	www
Inventory control	√		Agent software e-mail EDI

You've built it, but will they come?

The minute your site is downloaded, you have around 20 to 70 seconds to retain attention. This figure is decreasing because so many other Web businesses are on-line. This 'e-plosion' of Internet business, (if left unchecked) could lead to the downfall of small to medium sized organisations.

To stay on-line longer, understand the systems which secure your cybermarketing presence such as equipment, Internet Service Providers, website maintenance distribution and so forth. Even if you are only concerned with the shop-front part of your website – at the very least, you need to understand why a cybercitizen would want to visit your page. Keeping them hooked takes strong personalisation in what is, superficially, a highly impersonal mass broadcast media.

Summary

People access the Web to share ideas globally. They become part of the overall context of the message being conveyed and so share the experience of your cyber brand.

The greater the number of targeted surfers who log on to a website for a trusted brand, the higher the so called 'eyeball' share. To retain a surfer's attention you need to tailor and support a brand experience. The first way to establish trust of a cyberbrand is through security assurance. Technologies to protect data over the web are improving by the month. Initiatives from credit card companies to underwrite purchases over the Internet are ensuring that people feel more confident when dealing on-line with their favourite brands.

Cyberbrands are also taking advantage of greater bandwidths for faster downloads – reassurance for surfers who expect a prompt and relevant service from their favoured cyberbrand.

In terms of on-screen advertising, rich media banner ads increase cyberbrand awareness in a one-to-one dynamic environment. Rather than simply promoting a cyberbrand on a static banner advertisement, information is being disseminated and subsequent sales secured instantly at the click of a mouse.

Finally, however great your cyberbrand may appear on the screen, the ability to fulfil orders promptly through improved distribution systems ensures that surfers come back.

The more people linked to your network, the greater the opportunities to reach micro-communities with highly specialised interests. As the week progresses, we'll look at how easy it is to attract such 'Net Heads'.

The cybermarketing.com mix

Today we explore how cybermarketing affects your traditional marketing mix.

Business objective	Traditional marketing	Cybermarketing	Future marketing
Segmentation	Demographic lifestyle	Behaviour	Complex data
Recruitment	Advertising/agent	On-line	Direct cabled or wireless access to prospective employees.
Positioning	Local/national broadcasting/ publishing	Local understanding – global awareness	Service segmentation according to customer needs
Advertising	'Pulling' customers to the message	'Pushing' the message to customers	Empowering customers to 'push' or 'pull' at will
Education	Content led	Content and context led	Interactive
Distribution	Middle man	On-line – on target	One to one
Media	By classification	By interoperable platform	By digital and newer technologies
Administration	Paper based	Wire based	Multi-media based

Business objective	Traditional marketing	Cybermarketing	Future marketing
Branding	Market share	Share of customer 'eye-ball' share – number of surfers	Mind share – Or via web browsing, 'search-share'
Market reach	Geographic	Cybergraphic	Intellectual ingress

Get techie

Until recently, whenever marketers featured the Internet or indeed any computing application as part of the marketing mix, the lead was placed firmly in the hands of technical system integrators. Today, you have to be a marketing communications integrator. In doing so, decide from a practical business view how the Internet helps establish, maintain and enrich your market's attention ('eyeball share') and, ultimately, allegiance.

To be implemented successfully, cybermarketing needs to be:

- *planned* with your own aspirations in mind
- *organised* in collaboration with technicians
- *designed* in agreement with management goals: these could include extending your product life cycle or increasing the share of your customers or total market
- *managed* to enhance the long-term relationship between your organisation and its public
- *directed* by your marketing team, supported by technicians
- *measured* according to time, value, aspirations as well as management intent.

If you are not completely sure of what your cybermarketing campaign should achieve, you'll invariably end up with a compromise of several half-hearted stabs rather than a precise cyber hit.

Boxing clever

Every service or product coming onto a market can be categorised into one of four quadrants within a framework called 'The Boston Box'. The vertical axis of the box represents market growth, whilst the horizontal shows market share. Growth varies according to market demands and economic conditions. Companies falling in the best performing part of the matrix have products with a high market growth and share. These are called 'Stars'. Those with high market share but low growth are 'Cash cows'. In cases of low market share but growing as a whole, you get 'problem children' (also known as 'Wildcats' or 'Question marks'). Products struggling with low market share and growth are 'Dogs'.

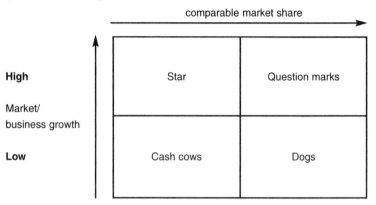

The classic Boston matrix

Carving your cybershare

Here's the conventional model adapted and updated for today's cybermarketing trends.

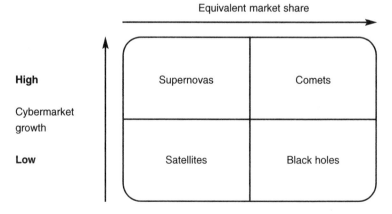

The modern Cyber matrix

To a greater or lesser extent, your cyber brand portfolio will spread across one or more segments.

Black holes
'Black Holes', the equivalent of 'Dogs', produce relatively little cash flow. If they are part of an external market, 'Black hole' surfers typically skim through sites at two clicks per page, occasionally lingering. However, that's as far as they go.

Satellites
If your cyber product or service enters Satellite cyber space, you'll be in the company of enterprises enjoying regular Internet traffic. As WWW watchers, 'satellite' surfers may visit sites offering services like books on-line, or audio/MP3 (audio file compression). As the market is mature, add value through enhancements such as useful information repositories or webcams at important events.

Satellites should be rewarded with beneficial features and values that they would naturally expect from your brand as conveyed in traditional advertising but reinterpreted for the cyber age.

Useful cyber innovations for Satellite markets may include:

- Free software to enhance printing of web pages
- Personalised Internet ordering
- Ongoing recommendations at discounted prices.

Comets
Comet sites may feature all the latest enhancements, but you'll still need to invest heavily in PR, links to other sites,

as well as traditional advertising, to increase market share in what is a very fickle sector.

Supernovas
Supernovas are at the pinnacle of cybermarkets. Popular search engines like Yahoo are Supernovas. However, be forewarned – competing organisations are always at your heels. You'll need to mollycoddle your market. For Internet Service Providers (ISPs), this includes delivering '24–7' support. For Internet businesses, ensure the backbone infrastructure, such as servers and software for internal networks as well as external, is current.

Is the Internet *really* profitable?

At the launch of the music company *MP3.com* on the stock market, the company was valued at 4.5 billion dollars. Yet by its third month, it had lost 1.5 million. That's not as gloomy as you may think. Internet companies are still brave pioneers. They, and hopefully you, are building the infrastructure and new commercial ethics of what in just a few years will be the dot.com standard. For now, economists value web companies by 'burn-rate' – the amount they lose. The idea is that the more money they lose, the more they have to lose – so the bigger they are! At the time of writing, the biggest cyberstore is Amazon.com.

Get cyberbranding

The pace of the Internet is forcing brand leaders to reassess their strategies in a bid to turn current modest brands into future global icons.

(Source – Newsweek)

Thanks to the Internet's incredible ability to personalise a global branding positioning, cybermarketing helps globally respected names become more relevant for local markets. The greater a cyberbrand's relevance, the more it reflects consumer aspirations and values. There are ten stages to founding powerful cyberbrands:

1 Establish a market need
2 Create market awareness by addressing that need
3 Form a point of distinction between you and your competitors
4 Make your brand memorable on the Internet – so it becomes a resource
5 Demonstrate value added innovations that enhance your basic fulfilment proposition

6 Encourage customer loyalty rather than one-off 'click and buy' sales opportunities

7 Support brand values with promotions, including press, banner advertising, PR and direct marketing

8 Re-invigorate your brand according to market conditions – without compromising your competitive point of difference

9 Offer a broad bandwidth to make your brand accessible

10 Support your cyberbrand presence with traditional marketing techniques.

The next generation

'First generation' sites purely supplied previously published marketing information and company background information. This included lists of products and financial status. These were, and still are, known as 'brochureware'.

Your Web presence should offer accessible and useful additional support and services to your market. However, if you want to feature your corporate brochure as part of a website, divide its content into logical sections, then save those sections as PDF files. As you've divided the brochure into manageable 'chunks,' downloading won't freeze your surfer's computer.

Cyber tip
Save pictures that don't have to be bigger than 25% of your individual web pages as low-resolution graphics. This improves downloading. Also, avoid complicated graphics for backgrounds. Pale colours work best.

Step	Internet	Extranet	Intranet
1. *Brochureware*	Cost effective publishing	Gets material to key people faster	Easy to control
2. *Add interactive features* e.g. e-mail	Encourages a simple relationship	Lets you issue/take simple instructions	Develops existing e-mail infrastructures
3. *Replace cumbersome distribution systems with cyber-based processes* e.g. on-line payments	Shortens time to market	Saves on administration	Encourages mobile computing on the road or at different locations
4. *Replace two-step systems with total cyber-based processes* e.g. distribution management	Offers a fast, tailored delivery service for customers on a global scale	Employs 'Just In Time' management techniques – this delays ordering goods from suppliers or warehouses until there is sufficient customer demand, so saving stock holding and handling costs	Saves on manpower

Four steps of Web business evolution

Trust me on this

The volume of information on the Internet tends to expand according to the number of people connected to the network (currently on target to reach 500 million by 2003). This throws up all kinds of implications:

- Specific information becomes harder to track down as it is drowned in a sea of facts
- The integrity of the information becomes increasingly dubious as anyone can publish anything
- The demand for information imposes significant pressure on technology to keep communication channels 'open' and 'flowing'.

Address these issues and you'll be well on the way to being respected as a valuable cyberbrand.

Search and you will find

In addition to Internet marketing techniques which elevate your information up the ranks of traditional 'spider' search engines (see Saturday's chapter), consider less obvious yet essential cybermarketing support tools.

For example, use software which manipulates and keeps your information relevant to your market. Equally, have an appropriate army of servers or datacenters. These computers deliver services to other computers on your network. Simple datacenter technology keeps everyone on-line thus ensuring that your marketing communication remains accessible, secure and available.

Get to the point
When dealing with either internal or external Internet markets, it is imperative that your site is designed not to lose surfers by thrusting complex mazes of 'dead-end' information at them.

Pornography sites, accounting for ten per cent of web pages and worth around $1 billion a year, are renowned for this. According to Media Matrix, in 1999 workers were spending 91 minutes a month viewing around 409 different pages. Just over half the time was spent devoted to viewing pornography.

Typically, porn sites throw up page after page of the equivalent of brick walls. When 'clicked', these lead to further sister pages, ultimately returning to the original content page. 'Regular' sites far too often use this incestuous activity. Such unwieldy Internet features are called Octopus or Loose-End sites. Avoid building them.

Cyberbrands – sites for sore eyes?

Arguably, external market facing sites that deal directly with customers, thus cutting out the middle person, alienate your conventional sales channel. I disagree. Your website could be used as an advertising support mechanism rather than a direct sales device. For instance, you could run a press advertisement for a new range of clothing. Meanwhile, you decide to generate traffic to your website. So the advertisement features your WWW address.

If, having accessed your site, all the surfer sees is an animated version of the same advertisement, you would have wasted a customer's time. However, if for example the site features a virtual catwalk of models wearing your range of clothing, you add real value. Add the addresses of local retailers and you will also keep your sales channel happy.

You may want to go the full distance by selling directly on the superhighway. This kind of e-commerce is simply another outlet that provides convenience for customers. Your traditional sales channel needn't worry too much. There will always be a demand for the sales cycle of some products and services to be completed in person. Even if your site doesn't generate instant sales, with the right exposure it still generates awareness.

Supporting your brand message, and so the profit potential of terrestrial retailers, is one of the Web's finer attributes. Newspapers and magazines use the Internet to offer up-to-the-minute coverage of news, or to provide an on-line search of previously published articles. In doing so, the paper reaches an audience beyond the familiar news-stand. Many broadcasters offer free access to the Internet, not to generate immediate sales but to spread cyber brand awareness.

Service companies can demonstrate that a brand is 'fresh' in its approach towards individualising its portfolio of benefits for customers. For example, insurance companies often offer personalised quotations via the Internet.

One thing that should always be borne in mind – building an on-line shop is quite different from building a cyberbrand. On-line shopping is about selling at every opportunity, even after the goods have been 'placed' in the electronic shopping cart. For example, rewarding the surfer for their custom with further discounts. Or recommending products to previous customers based on their preferences or buying patterns. On-line shopping is expected to be worth around £330 billion by 2002 (source: BBC). While the shopping experience should be based on retailing principles, reflecting marketing strategies, the brand experience should be based on marketing strategies which, depending on your long term goals, may or may not be manifested through an on-line shop.

Will the Internet eventually turn all retailers into dot.com sites? Traditional retailers with a dual presence on the street and Internet use technology to add value to their high street outlets. This may be through cyber cafes or e-catalogues that directly or indirectly enhance a retail image.

Yet it could be argued that consumers will rebel against the virtual world, in preference for returning to simple traditional modes of shopping and everything that this brings with it, like traffic jams and battling against hordes of shoppers. It would be like restricting the scope of your shopping experience to visiting a few small retailers, with limited stock on a high street, as opposed to a shopping mall's worth of choice, from hundreds of various retailers, all under one roof.

CYBER F@CTS

ACCORDING TO MORI, 10% OF ALL UK SURFERS DESCRIBE
THEMSELVES AS REGULAR ON-LINE SHOPPERS. THIS FIGURE
TENDS TO DOUBLE EVERY YEAR.

Go the distance

Software such as Java, Sun Microsystem's universally
adopted mother tongue of network computing, lets you
'push' your marketing message through any platform or
device including PCs, Macs, workstations, UNIX machines,
network computers, set-top boxes, palm held devices, wrist
watches or cellular phones.

To ensure that your message reaches your mobile audience,
using WAP technology sponsor a mobile news service for
cellular users. News can be accessed initially in a text
message form. While the mobile phone user is reading the
latest news, your message could be transmitted and
personalised according to the location of the phone, for
example you run a restaurant chain and want to direct
mobile phone users towards your nearest restaurant.
Loyalty is often influenced by convenience, so this kind of
personalisation enhances your business. It all amounts to
further integrity for your organisation and bigger dot.com
business opportunities all round.

Ports in a storm

The fusion of traditional marketing and new media
establishes even more powerful cyberbrands – some of

which start life on the Web. Micro cyber companies operating from a small office may use the Web to reach national or even international markets. As with all markets, the enterprises that offer the best value in terms of cost, audience appropriateness, service and access ultimately squeeze out the competition. The current trend is for large, established off-line brands to develop so-called 'Enterprise Information Portals'. These lead to anything related to the portal's theme, such as news or fashion brand sites.

In a nutshell, portals provide content from multiple sources. Themed portals evolved from Search Engines that traditionally pointed the surfer to any site with registered details. Portals generate targeted 'hits' and cash for website owners who:

1 want to be listed on the portal
2 want to advertise on a portal's banner space.

CYBER F@CTS

SOME PUBLISHERS USE PORTALS TO CAPTURE 'CYBERGRAPHIC' DATA. THIS MAY INCLUDE TRACKING HOW MANY 30-YEAR-OLD FEMALES VISIT A SPECIFIC SITE. WHAT DO THEY BUY, AND SO ON? THIS INFORMATION IS FURTHER ANALYSED FOR WOULD-BE INTERNET AND PRINT ADVERTISERS.

Portal flavours
A so called 'horizontal portal' presents information organised according to categories. Surfers are induced to return to such horizontal portals through associated services like investment market news, music news and so on.

Typically, a horizontal portal features:

- Web searching
- reference-news guides
- on-line shopping
- freebies like e-mail and community networking.

To further seduce surfers to a horizontal portal, many have negotiated with browsers like Netscape and Explorer to feature a special 'My Portal' button, eg 'My Yahoo'. When 'clicked' the surfer arrives at a specific portal.

The surfer can customise all such links to ensure receipt of a daily horoscope for instance. If precisely targeted, horizontal portals offer cybermarketers invaluable direct marketing opportunities. Some cybermarketers offer part of their site content to portals in exchange for links. For instance, newspapers may offer headline news in exchange for promoting the portal's URL in their publication and website. If you are going to consider a link exchange, simply send an e-mail to prospective link sites clearly explaining your URL and offer to link. You can find out more details from www.linkexchange.com

---

Cyber tip
Similar to portals, a 'trailblazer site' leads to useful support companies and tools via hypertext links. The better the tools, the greater your credibility as a valuable resource (See www.ineedcreativity.com).

Vertical Portals

It was bound to happen. Cybermarketers representing international news and special interest companies like TV stations eventually decided to create their own discreet portals.

Vertical portals are so individual that in some instances they are adapted as corporate specific Intranet portals, carrying a secure flow of company-wide information. The same idea works for Extranet business-to-business portals.

Thanks to thin-client computing architecture, the whole process of setting up portals is more affordable than ever. Thin-client computers don't require disk storage, applications or even operating systems. So they can include devices like mobile phones, screen phones and handheld organisers. All the essential information and software resides on a server, ready to be delivered as required to any Java protocol-enabled client.

Another benefit from vertical portals is that rather than investing large sums in advertising on search engine owned portals, you can build your own portal presence.

Portals – controlling your internal market

Portal technology offers fast, secure access to personal e-mail, data, applications, internal sites and network services from any Internet-connected device. The entire environment is web-enabled, so there are vast savings when upgrading individual applications. You no longer need to build a virtual private network. Research shows that it costs two and half times more a year to support 2,000 remote access users using traditional remote access infrastructures than through Internet remote access.

The right portal supplier can show ways to allow authorised users like employees to securely access network resources via a standard browser on any Internet-connected device like a palm or laptop computer. The business benefit of this is that you remain in total control of who enters from the Internet and what they can access. There's no need for special client software. Extranet business partners (behind a firewall) can also access authorised partner applications from any device with Internet abilities.

Portals – as you like it
Decide which level of portal sophistication is appropriate for your business needs.

Simple
- Company information
- Product and service data
- Search

Fundamental
- Company information
- Advanced Search
- Product and service data
- Company-wide directories
- Complex information
- Personalisation

Elaborate
- Company information

- Complex information
- Company-wide directories
- Customer support
- Channel collaboration
- Product and service data
- Advanced search
- Personalisation
- Transactions
- Personalised work management

Premium
- Supply support chain management
- Advance personalisation
- EDI (Electronic Data Interchange) stock control, with links directly to suppliers
- Java and associated software enabling

Cyberbrand or fad?

A cyberbrand has to be more than a 'cyberfad'. Compared to 'streetwise' fads, 'Web-wide' fads put vogue trends (like Star Wars, for instance) to shame. Left under-marketed, the average life cycle for a cyberbrand is from nine weeks to just under nine months.

How can you measure the power of your cyberbrand?

- **Cyberbrand extent**: integration of traditional brand values with Internet enabled technologies
- **Cyberbrand breadth**: market sector admiration through utilising Internet technologies to enhance perceived brand benefits

- **Cyberbrand influence**: the relevance the cyberbrand attracts from various market segments, including employees via intranets, suppliers via Extranets and shareholders via WWW
- **Cyberbrand affinity**: the allegiance your cyberbrand attracts from existing as well as likely customers
- **Cyberbrand alliance**: the degree of feeling and emotions evoked by your cyberbrand.

Enduring cyberbrands understand markets. In so doing, they enhance the conduct of cyber business. This includes the management of bandwidth issues. After all, no one wants to wait minutes for a webvert to download. It also means doing more than just plastering pages with brand logos. Such icons alone (that can't be identified by search engines) have no substance. Customers won't wait. Your brand may capture attention, but simply on its own it may not encourage loyalty.

This brand value approach extends to the placement and rationale of banner advertisements. There's no point featuring a banner ad if, once clicked, it doesn't lead anywhere that is relevant to the original content of the page or site where it first appeared. By approaching your cyberbrand from a customer point of view, you'll connect to your market's consciousness.

Cyber tip
Make 85% of your cyber strategy value-led and 15% sales oriented.

New Cyber e-conomics mix

Product

On-line support

Consistent reviews

Clearly designed (Web page)

Highly interactive

Surfer/customer-centric rather than corporate-centric

Place

Electronic distribution

Greater control of your supply
    management chain via: www.

E-mail

Intranet

Internet

Extranet

Improved enterprise-wide
    communication via Network
    computing devices: mobile
    phones.

Laptop computers.

Desktop computers

New customer value added
    opportunities via Jini activated
    household appliances (e.g.
    intelligent fridges, cookers)

Web screen phones

Electronic kiosks

People

Innovation

Vision

Dynamism

Logic

Style

Intuition

Technical Competence

Price

Secure credit card payment

Direct debit

Local billing

Promotion and e-branding

WWW offers

Brand-led site imagery

Intranet employee offers

Web banners

'Push-mail' (you send updates,
    rather than wait for enquiries)

On-line sales (customer sales
    enhancements' e.g. electronic
    'shopping carts')

Posters

Press advertising

Radio

TV

Direct mail

Web-shots

Web page sponsorship

Web newsletters

Process

Bandwidth management

Distribution

Ordering cycles

Mind your Ps

The original marketing mix, coined by Jerome McCarthy, was known as, 'the 'Four Ps'. This was amended to the 'Five Ps + *People*' and then 'Six Ps + *Process*'.

As no market ever stands still, the mix is constantly re-balanced as the cyber e-conomics mix demonstrates on page 39.

The Sun-Netscape Alliance – *www.neteconomy.com* – offers the following advice:

- Design your company around customers' needs
- Maintain dialogue
- Customise products and services
- Think beyond core product, ie more about the total customer experience and needs
- Don't fear organisational change – embrace it
- Manage your business in real time and offer 24–7 service
- Use the Internet to expand brand values and/or build an entirely new brand
- Expect change, plan and react accordingly
- Learn new skills – what you know is more important than what you own
- Use the Internet to reduce development time of new products and services
- Streamline the supply chain (Enterprise Resource Planning – ERP, which helps optimise every link in your chain)
- Offer greater customer convenience
- Wire your company for profits – consider customer imperatives and use your IT infrastructure to service external needs.

DOT. COM CLIENT

DOT. COM PATRON

DOT. COM CUSTOMERS

Reward patrons who spread the word on your behalf. The more people whom they can recommend the greater the mutual benefits. To ensure fair play, all the patron has to do is provide an e-mail contact for the new business prospect. Once the prospect becomes a customer, the patron is rewarded.

From brochureware to customer awareness

In Monday's section, I explained that many e-commerce businesses initially used the Web for brochureware. This step is aimed at those dot.com suspects we've just looked at. Getting people to browse through brochureware can be encouraged through traditional advertising, search engine marketing or good old fashion word-of-mouth. Once they've seen your brochureware, your audience will invariably demand more substance from your site.

The second stage is the information 'push' channel. Push technology can be likened to the dating game. You could either wait all night to make a move on your intended date or take the initiative through starting a conversation. If your opening gambit isn't sufficiently planned and styled you could end up dateless, spending the rest of the evening chewing on cheese puffs in the kitchen. Through empowering the person you want to 'chat-up', push technology puts you in control. He or she calls the shots for information, rather than you being forced into making an unsolicited approach.

This is great for customer support issues. Take the example of phone helplines. You can manage your customer support traffic by logging which enquiries attract the most 'hits'. Alternatively, you can feature a Web-customer support site in conjunction with a traditional phone-support site, thereby offering greater choice and further promoting a personalised service.

Finally, you can use 'kiosk-enabled' technology. This is embraced by organisations like local authorities who want to reach the community at the touch of a button: from offering on-line payment of community tax, to delivering the latest jobs from a strategically placed kiosk at either a town centre or bus shelter, for example. Such advances provide a novel advertising medium for cybermarketers.

A safer sale

People increasingly 'click and buy'. It saves time and hassle. However, the more clicks you request, the more reasons for surfers to 'click out' and move onto a less tedious site. So sell from the first click.

Web technology can go a long way to guaranteeing a no-fuss sale. In the past, to close a sale most companies offered a telephone number or a fax service. As any salesperson can tell you, once customers leave the premises, you have an uphill struggle to get them back. Today most companies offer secure on-line credit card payment services. This is made safe through technology called Secure Socket Layer Protocols which scrambles information to and from a computer over the open Internet.

Internet security concerns often centre on the confidentiality and integrity of data whilst in transit over the network. As the volume of Internet commerce rises, so the need has grown for virtual equivalents of real world commercial validity protection such as signatures, contracts, authorisation, liability, and dispute resolution. Digital signatures use security technology to provide certification and to offer a guarantee that the surfer is whom he or she claims to be.

Some cybermarketers offer on-line research for a limited time trial. This is fine, but credit card details are usually requested up front before any research can be conducted. The idea is that charges are debited only if and once the surfer decides to purchase the full service. More often than not this technique puts off more people than it attracts.

Cyber tip
You've got nothing to hide. Always feature your regular postal address on the site. Also, without consistent marketing no one will know that you're Web-active.

PRACTICE SAFE SALES

Hold your customers' hands

Having secured your e-customers, ask what they feel about your site. In so doing, you can build and segment specific customer profiles. Each group's comments contribute towards developing your Web presence by clarifying and enlightening your own ideas on ways and means to tailor your service.

The dot.com community

Call it the global or cyber village – both suggest a sense of community. Successful communities live and work in partnership. Your 'customer facing' site is a micro community of customers and suppliers. Help customers help each other via chat rooms and bulletin boards. Let them share a communal rapport with other communities. This could include offering freebies like T-shirts featuring your site, mouse mats – anything that helps spread not just the news that you are on-line but the feeling of good will. And remember, when a dot.com Patron gets in touch you should reply, not simply out of courtesy but with the aim to show that you are listening, reacting and collaborating to ensure a sustainable value-added cyber relationship.

CYBER F@CTS

WHEN E-MAILED BY POTENTIAL CUSTOMERS, 50% OF UK COMPANIES DID NOT RESPOND TO A REQUEST FOR INFORMATION. OF THOSE THAT DID, AROUND ONE THIRD DID NOT PERSONALISE RESPONSES. (SOURCE: UNIVERSITY OF WEST OF ENGLAND)

Putting it briefly

What are your dot.com marketing objectives? For example, informing customers about your new e-service, preparing and adapting your marketing collateral, updating your customer support systems and so on. Put all these requirements – and more – onto paper.

Your cybermarketing position
Your site reflects your organisation's personality. Like all personalities, it is multi-faceted, offering different qualities of service to different types of customers. Over time, these qualities mature. As a regular marketer, you ensure that your traditional advertising consistently reflects your personality. So the first impressions you make with customers mirror your organisation's inner strengths. This logic must be carried throughout your cybermarketing-positioning plan. Through distinguishing your dot.com

goals you can look at: Web business objectives, Web market objectives, Web competitive strategy.

Web business planning brief

Your dot.com business objectives

1. Why do you want to want to go into cyberspace?
2. What do you know about similar organisations in cyberspace?
3. Are your competitors on the Web?
4. Rate out of three, the applications used by your competitors, e.g brochureware.
5. What business aspect do you want the Web to address?
   For example:
   • Lead generation   • Departmental integration
   • Stock control   • Product distribution
   For each of these aspects, what results do you anticipate in the:
   i) short term?   ii) mid term?   iii) longer term?

Your enterprise-wide dot.com objectives

6. Who, at which stage and at what level of involvement, from planning to implementation and finally support, will need an input into your cyber plan? The following checklist will help to identify the relevant factors within your organisation.

Department	Planning (level: 1–4)	Implementation (level: 1–4)	Support (level: 1–4)	Who holds ultimate department responsibility?
Recruitment				
Finance				
Sales				
Distribution				
Brand marketing				
Product marketing				
Customer care				
Purchasing				
Corporate management				
Administration				
Research and development				
Training				

It is essential that you have the appropriate business financial systems to successfully manage your site. Seek advice from an e-commerce accountancy specialist who can explain the implications of local country tax and financial planning issues. Try www.nymanlibsonpaul.co.uk.

The fuller WWW cybermarketing brief

This self-contained brief covers every key question for developing a creative cybermarketing solution.

1. Who's going Web-wide?
Company name only. Other facts should be confined to a section called 'Background'.

2. Describe what you do
Telecoms, Financial, Manufacturing etc.

3. What should your budget cover?

- Site design
- Technical support
- Web-marketing
- Site copy
- Traditional support marketing

Remember: part of your budget should be set aside for unforeseen items.

4. In terms of site style, do you need:

- a new information site?
- an interactive site?
- a customer facing site?
- an internal market site?
- a business-to-business site?
- a combination of some or all of the above?

Would you consider:

- Incentiveware, e.g. free shareware (payment free software)?

- Screensavers, chat rooms?
- Databases of previously published e-zines, newsletters or data sheets?

5. Who will administer the site?
Do you need a specialised Web Master, i.e. a person who oversees the site?

6. Who will host the site?
See the section in Wednesday's chapter on ISPs and IHPs

7. Will you need multi-media CD ROM/DVD?

- With interactive access to the Web
- Stand alone

8. Web banner ads

- Why advertise?
- Should it be Web-marketed to other sites?
- Would you consider swapping banner ads with other related companies?
- Where should a banner ad lead, i.e. who hosts the end site?
- Should the Web banner be animated? If so by means of which language?
  (Bear in mind platform interoperability issues)
- How much do you want to spend on your banner ad?
- How will you measure the response to a banner add?
  For example number of impressions (times it appears over a fixed period) or actual clicks.

9. Media/PR access link

- How often will news be updated?

- Do you need a journalist 'hot-link' e-mail button?
- Will you offer a repository of press-releases and/or sound or video clips?

10. What do you specifically expect your site to achieve? By which of the following will you measure success?

- Return visits to the site
- Sales
- Postal savings
- Depth of knowledge discovered via e-forms
- Brand awareness
- Savings on existing commercial infrastructure
- Customer referrals/ leads
- Savings in paper-work
- Redirected enquiries via hypertext links and referrals
- Captured e-mail details
- Savings in human resources
- PR
- Awards for your site
- Distribution/asset management cost savings, eg via on-line auctions

In relation to your existing marketing plan what are your:

1 Cybermarketing tactical objectives?
2 Corporate strategic objectives?

11. About your Cyber community

- How Internet aware is your community?
- How often do they connect?
- Demographics
- Reasons for connecting?

Typical surfers connecting to your dot.com business:

- Staff
- Salespeople
- Distribution channel
- Retailers

- Journalists
- Suppliers
- Potential employees
- Shareholders

- Lobbyists
- Schools
- Students
- Partners

Name two requirements of each group.

12. How do you see yourself?
What style should the look and copy for your site adopt eg serious, casual?

13. What supporting media will you use to promote your site?
For example, national newspapers, PR trade press. In all cases, try and include a sample.

13a. Why did you opt for this media?

14. What Web marketing methods will you consider?

- *Meta-tags*: HTML – Hyper Text Transfer Protocol description labels which are 'read' by search engines
- *WWW advertising*: including banner advertising – small display ads on a site which, when 'clicked', link to your site
- Search engine marketing
- Links to other sites: via hypertext links which, when 'clicked', jump from the original page to another site or page
- Newsgroups: a public forum or discussion area on the Web
- Recipient approved e-mail
- On-line journalists

- Internal training
- Web rings: similar to Newsgroups, a band of home pages, with the same subject, grouped together by an organisation
- Mini sites modified in content according to target groups. These sites appear on appropriate complementary partner sites.

15. When do you expect to see:

- A draft?
- A published site?
- The support marketing campaign?
- The technical infrastructure?

Finally, sign off the brief. This binds you and your supplier to getting the project done as agreed and to a deadline.

BE WARNED: sites tend to grow in content according to the amount of time you spend building them. Time, especially when dealing with Web designers, is money. So agree everything on paper before committing to a Web publishing stage.

Never be tempted to squeeze additional last minute material into your site, especially after the initial contents have been agreed. You will exceed your budget and may compromise the integrity of your site's design.

Cyber tip

What are competitive sites offering? What is easy to download? Could you combine features from separate sites? How would you improve a feature? What would you design into your site that your competitors haven't?

Armed with this information, get yourself a roll of cheap plain wallpaper and flow-chart your site. Start with the first page.

- Indicate the number of featured pages, varying text throughout the site.
- Show links to other sites, i.e. hypertext links.
- Never offer too many links per page.
- Consider a permanent site flow chart on each page.

Back to the drawing board. Draw up a rough layout of each page, or an electronic draft version.

Samples of website layouts

Basic website structure

Basic customer dialogue site

Basic sales website

Establishing a WOW! site: the golden rules

- Ask someone not associated with your company for views on what makes a good site
- Establish what your site should accomplish before you start
- Make sure your site is relevant to your business
- Make sure your site features useful information
- Keep your site up-to date and spellchecked
- If possible make your site interactive
- Consider including a leisure aspect to your site
- Don't make your site too complicated to navigate
- Leave some budget for unforeseen changes
- Anticipate changes to your site format
- Develop your changes according to site performance
- Promote, promote, promote using traditional advertising and marketing techniques.

Establishing your position

Many organisations get their Web mission confused with their Web positioning. A mission is your vision of the future:

Within two years, we intend to switch our retail operation from traditional high street trading to 24–7 e-commerce.

Web goals adapt to changing long term circumstances. Once you have achieved your goals consider new missions and objectives.

Your positioning mirrors how your current dot.com service embraces targeted market needs, typically:

- What your site offers?
- How your Intranet/Extranet supports that offer?
- Why the offer is so special?
- How else you'll deliver a complete dot.com solution?

From position to mission

Position	Position	Mission	Mission
What you do	What you deliver	Where you want to be	Your perfect scenario, ideal position, ultimate achievement
Why you do it	How you deliver	How you intend to get there	

Solid ———————————————————————————————————▶ fluid

Questions to consider in your cyber positioning plan

1 **Why are you going on-line?** To reach a wider audience – to improve distribution cycles, to extend your connected enterprise to suppliers and partners and to gain greater control of your internal processes.

2 **How does Web-enabled technology enhance your business?** Your site delivers an easy way to order catering equipment, for example, or your Intranet offers greater management control.

3 **What makes your Web strategy a WOW! tactic?** Your WEBA: **W**eb, **E**nabled, **B**usiness, **A**dvantage.

For example, are you more Web savvy than your competitors? (WEBAs replace traditional Unique Selling Points)

Above all, for whom is your cyber business intended?

What specifically does this audience want?

Why should yours be the only Web business of choice?

What arguments can you add to substantiate your position?

Summary

- Establish a relationship with e-customers – make your site more valuable than 'brochureware'
- Explore ways to assure security for surfers – especially if you are going to sell on the Web
- Prepare a cyberbrief for outside creative suppliers
- Delegate to key personnel specific responsibility for your cyberplan
- Turn the average site into a WOW! site through following the golden rules and WEBA.

Your cyberhome
Internet hosting providers

In the short term, getting the right hardware and software for your 24–7 dot.com business may seem costly. However, in terms of longer-term savings covering every aspect from infrastructure to paperwork, the scenario may look a lot more encouraging. Plus, you have to consider the costs of your business being off-line if things are not sufficiently pre-planned.

HOME SWEET WWW

Companies like Sun Microsystems offer server solutions which scale according to your business needs. Beacon Group in Australia and Japan leads the world in Web-enabled temporal database management software such as Timecube which pin-points and tracks the historical performance of individual items in your database. Others offer relational databases, tools and application products, all vital for your cyber business plans.

In the right hands and with the right support, you can expand your e-commerce and open computing tactics from being a cost centre platform to a profit base, embracing selling, taking secure payments, encouraging customer/supplier relationships and reducing the buying cycle.

Cyber tip

If your customers prefer the option of secure Web payments, set up a special secure server and payment software program. At the very least, offer surfers the chance to print out a completed order form and fax or post it back. (A word of caution – don't copy the design of your non-cyber order form to the Web. You would be amazed at how many Web order forms feature the instructions, 'Please tear here'!)

Someone to watch over you

Diffusing your cyber business access amongst a network of several servers is called 'server farming'.

Apart from the expense of hardware and software, there is the cost of employing someone to manage your network. Depending on the size of your operation and the depth of your pockets, you can either pay for an on-site engineer or let an external host cover costs. Having your server and engineer on-site means you literally see everything as it happens. Providing of course that someone is there when 'it' does.

For example, if it's 3 am on a public holiday and your server goes down, it may still take hours to get into the office, assess the damage and then resolve the problem. On the other hand, if your site was hosted externally with a big Internet Service Provider you could spread the cost of hiring and action would be taken quickly.

Also keep in mind the outlay of installing and maintaining a host's main data cable into your premises. Many believe that the cost is justifiable as it speeds up network access times for employees. In theory, the bigger the bandwidth, the greater the amount of data. In practice it's how you manipulate the bandwidth.

To ensure your site remains efficient and reactive, instal a separate cable for secure, swift staff e-mail surfing, leaving all the bandwidth on your other line for your main site.

Your place or mine?

Internet Hosting Providers (IHPs) feature Virtual Web Servers. These computers offer access to several dedicated sites on one server. As there are only a restricted number of sites per server, you gain from an *a la carte* hosting service. You can load software remotely, as well as allow a host server to run programs on your behalf as an integral element of your Web connection on any kind of operating system. Arguably, with this option, only limitations are the amount of space allocated on a host server and on your disc drive.

One step beyond
If you prefer not to share server space with other organisations but equally you don't want to take up valuable office space with your own servers, consider co-hosting with

an IHP. Your site will be located and monitored at your host's main Internet access building. You can gain secure access to the server and negotiate to pay by the number of hits (volume of customer interest) you receive, or a flat fee that allows for unlimited traffic. This is one step below actually becoming your own ISP. Today, the option of being your own ISP isn't as expensive as you may believe. You can negotiate to market your own ISP name as a joint venture with an existing IHP or telecoms provider. This means that you can send out your own branded internet connection software which offers free Web access. Once the IHP or telecom company has made an agreed commission from the initial telephone calls to your service, you too can take a percentage share in future dial-up access telephone fees.

Final check list
Before taking the final plunge with any IHP, draw up a checklist:

- Traffic: Is there a restriction to the number of hits you can have? If so what are the extra costs?
- How much disk space can you have? For a powerful site look for anything from 50 Mb upwards.
- Can you have your own domain name?
- What if you want to move your site – are there any penalties?
- What kind of host service commitment can you anticipate?
- Can you speak to other customers?
- Can your host deal with all operating systems, including Mac, UNIX, Windows and NT?
- Can you personalise software for benefits like processing order forms (Common Gateway Interface

scripts which let you interface programs on your PC with servers, so you can add site information as you please)?

- Can you upload designs/new data to the site?
- Do you have to pay separately for e-mail?
- If you are dealing with an overseas country, does the host offer tailored local connections?
- Can the provider cope with geographic time differences and local peak demands?
- Is the provider in for the long term or quick profit (this will affect service contracts)?
- Can the provider support developments like Web TV?
- Does your host offer 'multihoming', i.e. more than one main link to the Web? This is essential: if one link fails other resources keep your site on-line.
- Can you get regular site visit reports?

Internet Service Providers (ISPs)

Also known as Internet Access Providers, these offer dial-up services connecting your organisation to the World Wide Web. Many also offer a hosting service, but this is not their main source of revenue. Providers managing infrastructure and bandwidth are called Internet Platform Providers.

Types of dial up service
If your company needs to connect no more than five PCs to the Web (mainly for e-mail, for instance), consider a standard 56 Kb modem connection per PC, over a standard phone line. Or for faster traffic or to use the phone and e-mail on the same line, perhaps a 128Kb connection; split by 64 Kb and 64 Kb. Either way, you pay a monthly subscription that covers unlimited Internet access.

In its favour, a regular monthly subscription is a cost-effective way to get connected. Apart from a phone point and modem there is no other hardware commitment. On the downside, though:

- it can be difficult to track site visitors
- phone bills can swell, especially with lots of accounts
- support can be sketchy
- unless you have a friendly ISP, updating your site contents can be difficult at best or impossible at worst.

Go with the flow

Once you connect over five computers, seriously consider investing in an Integrated Subscribers Digital Network (ISDN) supported by a router. If you want to send large graphic files to designers or printers, you really cannot do without an ISDN. Other benefits include:

- instant connections and disconnections, saving cost and time.
- a network of up to forty PCs can be connected to one ISDN line and still operate unremittingly
- you can allocate individual PC web addresses, perfect for guiding traffic as well as internal e-mail systems.

You could consider installing a dedicated high speed leased line. You pay for the line, not the charges, which guarantees a steady connection. Owning the line means you can dispense with an ISP. On the downside, weigh the costs (which are high) against your Web usage. Firewalls (security software) will have to be incorporated as your company is directly linked to the World Wide Web. You'll also need either to employ or have access to someone who can maintain your line 24–7.

The bigger your bandwidth the broader your marketing potential Cyberbrand leaders offer the biggest bandwidth – and thus the greatest Web service.

Something for nothing?

An ISP often provides free Web space along with free e-mail addresses and other goodies such as website statistics, tailored Portals (see section on Portals), community chat-rooms and on-line help.

However, you don't own a clearly personal Web address. Instead your address becomes part of the ISP's Web address such as **theworks@freespace.net** (these sites are called 'sub domains' or 'non virtual' accounts). Should you decide to move onto another service provider, you'll have to re-register your site: a nuisance when having to inform all of your customers about the new address.

Demand more from your Internet Service Provider
You are spoilt for ISP choice. By 1999 there were over 3,000
Western European ISPs. Don't automatically opt for the biggest
or most expensive ISP. The more people connected to an ISP the
greater the potential for Web congestion. On the other hand,
the more people connected to an ISP, the greater the chance that
customers are happy with the service. Take your choice!

In addition to the standard ISP services, your provider may
offer one or more of the following:

* Website development and training
* E-commerce such as electronic storefronts and on-
  line information services
* Intranet/Extranet hosting
* On-line marketing support
* Database hosting
* Premium network services; including Virtual Private
  Networks (VPNs)
* Reselling of hardware and software to corporate clients
* Voice over IP (the digital low cost, Web-enabled
  alternative to traditional telephone services).

When you've got to go

Service and disk space are the main reasons why people
move sites from ISPs and IHPs. If and when you decide to
move the transition should be made easier by taking the
following measures:

First, obtain a written agreement that permits release from the
ISP's service within a timeframe convenient to your business.

Secondly, make sure you check and complete all relevant

paperwork regarding the responsibility for the technical, administrative and financial aspects of your domain. If your domain name ends with .co.uk, .ltd or .plc, register details with an organisation called Nominet (*www.nominet.org.uk*). Come what may, you'll officially own the domain. And as with most other legal aspects of this ilk, ownership is nine tenths of the law. If you wish to register a dot.com address, amongst the places to try is *www.com-domains.com/*

Thirdly, always keep a back-up copy of your site on disc.

When it comes to moving the domain, simply inform the incumbent provider and successor, co-ordinate a day and time for the move, making sure your address provider is given sufficient notice – and then move.

Domain name 'landgrab'

Eventually, the Web will have to replace domain names with domain numbers. If not, the names will just get longer and longer. Today, www.sex.com is so profitable (with over nine million registered members) that it allegedly charges cybermarketers $1 million to place a monthly banner ad on the site. www.drugs.com in 1997 cost its owners $200,000 to buy. www.wallstreet.com sold for $1.03 million in 1999 and www.beer.com is valued at $7 million.

Summary

Today you learned to choose the appropriate means to connect to the Web for your business. Remember – consider the volume of anticipated Web traffic. Do you need to guarantee Web connect 24–7? Do you need to send documents more substantial than word processed e-mail – if so you'll need ISDN – and can you afford to host a server on site?

Cyber research

For an effective cybermarketing plan, you need to understand:

- Who wants your product or service?
- Why would they venture into cyberspace to find it?
- How can you prevent them from 'clicking' with your competitors?

The more you ask, the more you'll need to ask. Such as, what is the potential value of your cyber market? If you aim to sell, which of your products already performs well in a direct marketing context? All these affect your cyber marketplace. What about your cyber strategy?

- How will cybermarketing affect the end cost to the consumer?
- What are the best ways to control distribution?
- How do you exploit local issues globally?
- How will you manage customer support programmes?
- Can you provide an effective dot.com service?
- How do your competitors fair in all of this?

Published cyber research

Various firms produce cyber reports covering everything from who's on-line, to why they use the Internet. Report prices vary depending on their accuracy. There are also some on-line companies who are happy to offer basic reports free of charge. They do this as part of their own cybermarketing strategy. The free reports or newsletters encourage visits to the report writers' main site or to the sites of interest covered in the newsletter. Some enterprising cybermarketers charge the featured sites for the privilege to be included in the distributed e-mail reports. Find out more about the latest sources for such reports by e-mailing info@makemesuccessful.com

Search engine research

The most common method of research is via search engines. There are thousands of such engines on the Web, yet only a few are used extensively. For a comprehensive list of information sites try www.ineedcreativity.com.

Turbo charged research

The basic way to find a subject is to enter your keywords (in lower case format) in the 'SEARCH FOR' box, click the search icon and wait for the results. Then click on the link provided (underlined and in colour) which takes you to the site. Note that inputing in lower case finds both the lower and upper case versions of your desired subject.

If you want a specific word included in your search, put a plus (+) sign in front of the keyword in the search box:

creativity + works

To exclude a word and hence refine your search, place a minus (−) sign before the unnecessary word in the search box:

creativity + works − art

To enhance your search with different endings, type an asterix (*) at the end of the keyword:

Wish* – also finds wishes, wishful, wishbone, wishy-washy

Many search engines feature multiple choice, 'tick box' driven searches. However, some like AltaVista offer deeper searching abilities.

You type ...

domain:domainname	Finds pages with a specific domain
domain:org	Finds organisation pages
host:name	Finds pages on a specific computer
host:jonathan.theworks.co.uk	
	Finds pages on an individual PC called Jonathan at the works.co.uk
image:filename	Finds pages with images with a specific file name, eg image: menorah – finds all pictures of menorahs
link:URLtext	Finds pages containing the

	specified text in any part of the page other than an image, link or URL
title:text	Finds pages containing specific words or a phrase in the page title
<u>URL:text</u>	Finds pages with a specific word or phrase in the title
applet:calculator	Finds pages using applets (a free application program that performs a simple task) called calculator

Lap top research

The best source of on-line research is to ask for views from your existing circle of customers and associates as well as employees and suppliers. Surfers hate to waste time completing forms, so design a questionnaire which ensures uncompleted questions don't hold up form processing through re-posting, ie asking again for the form to be completed because of lack of information.

Next, think about why you are asking surfers to complete a questionnaire. What will they and you gain? Reassure surfers that answers are confidential, including a confidentiality clause before and after your questions. If you intend to use the answers for other divisions within your company, offer your respondents the option of declining to share their data with other related services (if any division is a separate company, normally, under the Data Protection Act, you are prohibited in the UK from sharing data without the correspondent's permission). For example: **This Net survey is anonymous. Answers are never written to disk. Plus of course we have no idea of your real identity. So please answer honestly.**

If specifically cited at the end of the research session, you may offer respondents a sales brochure on behalf of the company commissioning the research. But beware: covert, 'pushy' selling via Web research isn't just illegal but, from a marketing point of view, stupid. You'll probably alienate more potential customers instead of recruiting them.

Planning your questions
Make your first question easy, completing a sample question to show how to answer the rest of the questionnaire.

Ask one question at a time, eg NOT **Do you have a PC and MAC?**

Try whenever possible, to avoid open-ended questions, eg **Will cyberspace become more important to business than retail space?**

Opt for simple words rather than convoluted ones. eg NOT **expostulate** – instead **argue**.

Whenever possible avoid leading questions, eg **Do you surf at work because it is cheaper than surfing at home?**

Don't intimidate surfers, eg **Do your work mates think you're cool?**

CYBER F@CTS

BRMB INTERNATIONAL RESEARCH REVEALS THAT OF THOSE WHO ARE ON-LINE, 42% OF PEOPLE IN THE UK ACCESS THE WEB FROM HOME, WHILE 38% GO ON-LINE FROM THE WORKPLACE

Always offer a choice of answers to specific questions, including a NOT APPLICABLE option, eg **Do you have a Single PC [] More than one PC [] Are part of a network [] None of the above []**

Be wary of semantics. Don't use language which reflects your personal views, eg neither **Geek** nor **WebHead**. Rather **Web technologist**

Include a '**Don't know**' option where applicable. If the surfer doesn't have an opinion he or she may give up on your entire questionnaire. There are no 'right' answers. Assure your respondent you are assessing your product or service – not the surfer.

Limit the range of your questions. Rather than: **How many e-zines do you subscribe to?** ask about each of the e-zine categories by sector, one at a time and then: **In a month** do you get e-mail from **one [ ] two [ ] three [ ] e-zines?**

You can be guided further on how to ask a general research question by studying Teach Yourself Imaginative Marketing (Hodder & Stoughton Educational).

CYBER F@CTS

ACCORDING TO FORRESTER RESEARCH, 60% OF THOSE WEB VISITORS WHO START AN ORDER FORM NEVER COMPLETE IT. A GROWING TREND TO COMBAT THIS LETHARGY IS TO OFFER SURFERS A 'PHONE ME' BUTTON. THE CYBERMARKETER RECEIVES THE SURFER'S DETAILS, THEN CALLS BACK VIA A REGULAR TELEPHONE LINE.

Virtual Brainstorming™

One of the most innovative types of Web research is called Virtual Brainstorming™ (VB). Devised by *The Creativity Works*, it uses the Web as well as other media to generate an appropriate physical and psychological environment for solving problems. For example, rather than surfers just completing a questionnaire, they can explore a specially designed research site, 'click' on items of interest, answer a few questions – and control the research. All of this is supported by focus groups using creative problem solving methodologies.

VB media range from global conference-type links between participants, to the utilisation of Virtual Reality Modelling Languages, including Java and related 'Write Once – Use Anywhere' software. VB sessions may feature the physical simulation of either the specific problem to be brainstormed or areas relating to the problem. Typically, this would include the orchestration of sight, taste or touch. In all instances, VB features the talents of a trained facilitator, project co-originator and designer. You can find out more by visiting www.makemesuccessful.com

Cyber consumer targeting

Today, in the UK alone, over ten million consumers have direct access to the Internet. According to Fletcher Research, by 2003 there will be 20 million UK surfers, with 7.5 million connecting from home.

The stereotypical surfer is male, 35 years old, financially secure and living in a house without children. Male ABC1s

UK Internet penetration is approaching 50%. This is obviously an extremely sizeable and key potential market, but with so many people converging onto the Web generally, you need to rationalise how you segment a target audience.

How many on-line?
Based on published surveys, an 'educated guess' as to how many are on-line worldwide by mid 2000 is 181 million. These figures take into account that only 15% of the world's population contain 88% of all the Internet users and 80% of the world's population hasn't even used a telephone, never mind surfed the Web!

Sex
The broadest way to segment a Web audience is by sex. In 1994, male surfers outnumbered female surfers by four to one – now the numbers are close to being level, with women accounting for around 43% of the UK market (Source: MORI). According to NetSmart, 88% of US women

said the Web simplifies their lives. 83% said it saves time. 55% go on-line because it saves money. 81% of women said they don't know how they survived without the Internet.

In the UK, the growth of the Web has impacted on traditional segmentation methods to such an extent that the government has suggested dividing socio-economic groups into a hierarchy of job categories. (This can be downloaded from www.makemesuccessful.com).

Cyber tip
E-mail can double as an advertisement. Simply add a 'signature' file message (found under the preferences section of your e-mail program). Type any message you wish. Each time you send an e-mail the 'advertisement' follows. This is especially effective when participating in newsgroup discussions.

Newsgroups
To get closer to your cyber audience visit a newsgroup. There are thousands on-line. Each forum of surfers has specialised interests including your organisation's field. Through earning respect by targeted newsgroups – no more than eight really good ones – you can understand your market's character and with permission from the newsgroup controller, conduct informal research. To find your ideal newsgroup visit www.dejanews.com or www.ineedcreativity.com.

Web rings

Your site probably offers similar products and services to many others. Rather than fight the competition, why not join a Web ring? This is a collection of links with a common theme or interest which is actively sought by would-be customers via search engines. To find one that's suitable for you go to www.webring.org. Alternatively, start up your own, profiting from inviting other sites to link to your site.

CYBER F@CTS

JUPITER RESEARCH ESTIMATES THAT BY 2002 TEENAGERS WILL GENERATE $1.2 BN IN ON-LINE PURCHASES. CHILDREN AGED 5 TO 12 WILL SPEND $100M. BY 2005 THERE WILL BE AROUND 77 MILLION UNDER 18'S ON-LINE GLOBALLY. IN BRITAIN, A STUDY BY NOP RESEARCH FOUND THAT, SOCIALLY, SURFERS ARE DESCRIBED BY TEENAGERS AND CHILDREN (WITH AND WITHOUT INTERNET ACCESS), AS 'CLEVER', 'FRIENDLY', 'COOL', 'TRENDY' AND 'RICH'.

Summary

- Target your research
- Construct your on-line questionnaire with care
- Cybermarket to newsgroups and Web rings
- Check out Web-published material through search engines
- Consider the virtues of Virtual Brainstorming
- Pinpoint the characteristics of your surfers and serve them appropriately.

Cyber copy

Hey you! 'Click here'.

Your surfers simply don't have the time to trawl through a densely worded website or e-mail for valuable marketing propositions. Once people have logged onto your site your words need to keep them hooked. Vary the shape of the words on the screen. If a screen looks like a congested car park, you'll lose surfer traffic. Give words the space to breathe. Every word on your page is like a soldier in your cyber army. Each has the potential to infiltrate deep into your prospective audience's psyche. As a group, your words form a battalion of arguments that defend your cyber brand positioning. So command them well.

A common cybercopy mistake is to incorporate hypertext links into the middle of a sentence. Through clicking on the link, your reader never completes your sentence. You quite literally waste your words. Moreover, as in all forms of writing, people naturally read the beginning of your cyber copy, then lose interest, only to regain interest towards the end. There is a simple way to keep your cyber audience alert, and the clue is in your hands. This book is divided into seven days. That means seven separate triggers of interest. The more you can subdivide your message into readable chunks, the greater the chance of retaining a hold on your potential customers' minds.

Open minds – open opportunities

Whenever I write a business letter, I try to keep my reader's thoughts open. The same applies to cyber copy. The end of a paragraph signifies the end of a specific thought. That could be misinterpreted as the end of a message. The trick is to link each thought so that together they become a train of ideas.

'Open reading' is particularly challenging on the Web. When your surfer watches a screen (which they read from the centre outwards), there's nothing to fold up (like a piece of paper). Once the surfer gets distracted or tired, he or she is likely either to click out of your page or literally switch off. One way to avoid 'closed reading' is to feature link phrases that encourage the surfer to read further and longer:

'But . . .'	'What's more . . .'
'However . . .'	'In addition . . .'

You can also use Web technology such as animated GIFS (pictures) to lead the surfer through your site. Unlike any other form of advertising, cybermarketing technology delegates final control of content to your audience, so it's not enough to invest in mass 'wall-papered' awareness of your message/brand. Instead, consider why a surfer would choose to read or access that message in the first place.

Stuck on you
'Gluey bits' is a cybermarketing expression relating to features and benefits that keep surfers 'stuck' to your site. Crucially, these will ensure that your site contents are current and appealing.

Gluey suggestions
1 Feature a news section or updated database of useful facts.
2 Offer something a surfer can't get elsewhere – such as a special deal section.
3 Link to a site offering ready-made 'gluey bits' such as a financial newspaper's stock market page (speak to the paper for costs).
4 Offer rewards just for visiting your site (great to elicit e-mail addresses).
5 Personalise page preferences.
6 Intrigue with an interactive game or competition.

Have you read this?

Daily you listen or see up to 200 orders: 'mind the gap', 'visit this site' and so on. Twenty per cent are forgotten. So avoid cybernoise where a confluence of cyber messages drowns out the thrust of your well-intentioned argument.

Another potential downside of snappy cyber copy is that

> **Cyber tip**
> Competition rules vary depending on your server's
> location. If it is in the UK you may have to consider
> restricting entrants to UK citizens. EEC regulations
> apply if you want to make your competition Euro-wide.
> (Try www.europarl.eu. for help) You can learn more
> about competition and prize draw rules by studying
> Teach Yourself Creative Advertising and Copywriting,
> published by Hodder & Stoughton Educational.

we are becoming a nation of e-literates, uncaring for
grammatical style. So revert to the craft of getting your
message intelligently read. Rely on fundamental truths as
practised in traditional direct mail copy:

Attention leads to Interest, Interest leads to Desire, Desire
leads to the need for Conviction, and Conviction leads to
Action. (**AIDCA**). Paramount in this equation is Conviction.
Unless you can *convince* your cyber audience of your
proposition's value, cybercopy is just marketing 'garnish'.
Today's digerati can see beyond the pomp: they want
attainable benefits.

> **Cyber tip**
> Follow up an e-mail or completed e-form within 24
> hours. Any longer and you widen the gap towards
> securing a cybersale.

Cyber-grabbing words and phrases
Assess the following sentences:

A) Activate words and sentences – seize your surfers' attention.

B) The more active your words and sentences, the higher the probability of retaining your surfers' attention throughout.

Which sentence did you prefer? If it was A, you'll find the following cyber-grabbing words invaluable.

Tremendous	Money	Profit
Unbelievable	Huge	Celebrate
Mega	Congratulations	Sparkle
Remarkable	Fast	Saintly
Cool	Evil	Eternal
Wicked	Crème de la crème	Imagine
Explode	Oy!	Guarantee
Sexy	Free	Initiative

Cybermarketing e-mail 'grab' phrases like 'read this before your next coffee break' are always a good bet. But use them liberally to complement rather than replace a solid benefit-led proposition.

- Are you ready for this?
- Hate work?
- Want to meet your match?
- Do you really need to read this?
- Here's what you've been waiting for
- Save direct
- Haven't we met?

- Your competitor wants this kept secret
- I wish someone had told me ...
- Don't you just hate e-mail?

Avoid innuendo in e-mail headings. For example:

To: (name of recipient)
RE: Suck my pen ...

The surfer opens the message which reveals:

Sometimes, work gets me so frustrated that when I
suck my office pen, I swallow the ink! If you have days
like these, you'll be interested to learn about our brand
new ...

Also, avoid overt capitalisation in e-mails: OVER
EMPHASIS LOSES IMPACT, whilst *Italics* or **bold** may lose
format on the surfer's browser.

Beware vapourware
Vapourware is a type of software or website that promises
much but delivers morsels. Instead aim for substance in
your copy. Simply explain your product or service benefits:
When can you deliver ... Can you offer a guarantee? ...
Demonstrate a product's features and benefits through
words and in graphics if appropriate, including using
animated technologies like Flash and Java. As with all
forms of direct marketing, wherever possible use
testimonials from satisfied customers: no other form of
advertising does you greater credit than a personal
recommendation.

A case of déjà vu?
If you can't add anything new on the Web to your existing

marketing material, endeavour to rewrite your brochure, as if it were a storyboard.

Instead of subheads, use Web-animated technology and graphics to introduce new text scenes. Treat each screen page as if it were the only one a surfer sees. In many cases your site will only be read superficially. That's why copy has to work hard. Even if you feature hypertext links, assume your surfers will never explore further. When and if they do, your efforts to maximise impact will be especially rewarding.

As with all story outlines, make sure that your site has a beginning (intro or overview), middle (content – with substance) and end (either directing surfers to a sales/enquiry e-form, or ensuring that you've covered everything they need to know). To ensure they reach a conclusion, don't be afraid to offer some kind of reward for their completed e-form. Also highlight urgency for their early response.

Finally, spellcheck your site. Better still, get others to spell-check it and never rely solely on a word-processing spellchecker program.

Wave your banner

By the year 2002, according to ActivMedia, Web advertising revenue will be worth in excess of $43,300,000 annually.

Apart from search engines and traditional marketing tools – including word of mouth – the most common Web advertising is the banner ad. Originally, these static oblongs featured a JPEG or PICT graphic of a company logo. When clicked, the banner linked to a cybermarketer's site.

Advertising revenues were, and still are, generated by the site hosting the banner. Nowadays, in addition to being animated through rich media content such as Java and Flash, banners are personalised. So, as well as being branding devices, they are also direct marketing tools.

Banner personalisation is achieved on two levels. First, via the environment where the banner appears. The more aligned the host site is to your market, the higher the chance of someone clicking the banner. Check that you can track your clicks either via a specialist Web agency or using software tracking systems (go to www.advertpages.co.uk/list_advertising.html to find links to US and UK media agencies).

Good places to feature banners include e-zine listings, newsletters and what I call hand in glove sites. These are cybermarketers whose product or service complements yours. For example, an umbrella manufacturer and a weather forecaster. In either case, you feature a banner/personalised version of your site specific to surfers visiting the partner site.

You can also consider a part banner/part sponsorship of a site. For example, my own company, *the creativity works* (**www.theworks.co.uk**), was involved with a general Internet site for European soccer. The site was marketed as a sponsorship deal to cybermarketers. The idea being that rather than cybermarketers having to build their soccer site from scratch, one was ready-built. By advertisting on it they gained from being associated with a popular sporting event and avoided paying costly sponsorship fees directly to the event's official organisers.

Secondly, consider banner personalisation – a banner ad featuring a personalised link of value. For example, some banners double up as 'phone me' buttons. The surfer completes basic e-mail details, clicks the banner and receives a phone call from you.

You can join a free banner link network. Every time a surfer visits your site displaying a banner, you gain credits. After around two credits your banner is displayed on someone else's site. To find a list of exchanges go to www.advertpages.co.uk/list_ban.htm

Another technique is a free quotation based on some simple questions within the banner – for example, What's your name, age, are you a smoker? One click returns a basic life assurance quote. As you can imagine, the variations of this are endless. The only limits to banner flexibility – like most cyber creative issues – is bandwidth. The wider the bandwidth, the greater your creative possibilities.

One kind of banner ad that surfers either love or hate is the pop up box banner. This pops onto the screen whenever the surfer links to a specific site. It can either stay on the screen while the surfer continues browsing, 'flash' or stay a while and then fade. Pop up boxes – also known as Interstitial ads – are particularly effective as part of a search engine web marketing plan. The gateway appears before the engine sends a surfer to your site or a site related to the subject by keyword, dealt with by your organisation (see Sliding Doors in Saturday's chapter).

Superstitials, the next big thing in banner ads, feature Java-based rich media in any format: HTML, Director, Flash or GIF. Unlike conventional banner ads, the superstitial does not load until the browser has loaded the entire page. Their cost to cybermarketers can be up to four times the price of an ordinary banner, but they can yield up to twenty per cent better 'click through' rates.

Clicking for profit
The more popular the hosting site, and the more times your site appears, the bigger your banner budget (it's worth checking if your banner is going to be shown in rotation with other advertisers or 'fixed' to a specific page URL). Costs will modulate as more sites turn into portals. Another development, Web TV, with estimated audiences of 67 million in the US and Europe by 2003 (source: Datamonitor), may see the price of banner adds rocketing sky high or the price of traditional TV commercials falling. Even more so when, by 2015, TVs in homes may be 'hung' like wallpaper across entire walls, bringing a new dimension to the virtual world.

In the meantime, as an alternative to paying for a banner ad you could always host one – and still pick up valuable business.

Blip this!
An alternative to banner advertising is the Blipvert. Rather than sending a regular e-mail, a 30-second audio clip of a sound track is attached. This idea is being adapted as part of 'signatures' at the bottom of e-mails. Often, Blipverts feature radio commercials or music excerpts.

Summary

Today we looked at the importance of cyber-grabbing phrases. You discovered why you shouldn't opt for the first banner ad offer someone tries to sell you. Finally, you've been encouraged to make your banner ad interactive.

Climbing higher

I've left discussing how to improve your site search engine rankings until last. Most people assume that the business of cybermarketing is only about improving a site's visibility. As I hope I've shown, cybermarketing touches *every* aspect of your organisation, not just the obvious. Here then are some tips to take your site to within the top 10 rankings and so further enhance its WOW! potential.

Most Cybermarketers have already had some Internet exposure and now want to make their sites work harder. Start by assessing what your peers think about your site. If they really like it, they'll link. Go to *www.yahoo.com* and type:

link: (your site address URL)

and you'll see just how many other sites link to yours. To tune up your site, from improving browser compatability to the overall design, go to **www.websitegarage.com**. This shows useful ways to tune up your site, from improving browser compatibility to the overall design. (When considering 'visibility', check how your site looks on different versions of browsers – some may not support your software, hinder printing or compromise graphics.)

Keywords open doors

Search engines rank sites using certain parameters. Some individual sites bid for keywords. Some engines rank according to a site's popularity and number of links. Most commonly, engines rank according to frequency and position of keywords. Every day engines catalogue billions of keywords using an algorithm. Ranking often depends on elements like domain name, document title, HTML page description, page position, frequency and pattern of words, sentence and paragraph structure and other HTML mark up considerations.

Choose your words, carefully repeat them often (especially in the first two paragraphs) but not excessively throughout the site. Wherever possible, turn keywords into plurals or nouns. These will throw up more findings. (*cybermarketer* is better than *cybermarketing*).

www.rankthis.com and **www.positionagent.com** show where your site actually lies in the hierarchy of search engine listings. This is assessed by either your URL or keywords related to your business.

Every Web page has its own coding. To see your HTML code whilst on the Web, go to 'File' and then view page source. This is full of meta-tags. Meta-tags are the backbone search support behind every site. Agree with your colleagues on suitably descriptive keywords, including associated words. Remember: if you are selling lots of models from a portfolio of goods, always involve the model number as many surfers will look for this first. Check that in the code line starting

```
<meta name = 'keywords' content =
```

you've added the appropriate words. Another tip is to try and feature a keyword within your domain name. This further improves your ranking. Engines take note of words with a major heading format. So use pre-set formats like

Heading 1, 2 and 3.

Although search engines reward extra ratings for nice

graphics, without XML (see next page) their technology often cannot read pictures (that includes logos and features like animation). So, returning to your meta-tags, include an alt tag description wherever there's a picture. In this tag describe a benefit rather than simply writing – graphic. Bear in mind that the bigger your graphic file size, the longer the download. Try compressing your graphics, providing picture quality remains acceptable . If your site features an animated splashpage – featuring software such as Shockwave – surfers may not get to see it if they find your site via a search engine. As with the case of graphics, many search engine robots can't interpret frames or programs which surfers update when linking to the Internet (CGIs) – such as shopping carts. There are always new ways around this – consult your Web designer.

Engines are pretty dumb, often providing inappropriate results, so label tags intelligently. If your order form features columns of information, make sure that each column has a meta-tag relating to its content as opposed to format.

In 1999, W3C, the non-profit making Web standards group, suggested that cybermarketers start to use the new generation of HTML: XML (Extendible Mark-up Language). This tackles both Web content as well as categorising data according to agreed definitions. So 'Chips' would be signposted and made specific to either food or computers, 'The Times' would relate to a newspaper as opposed to clocks and so on. XML also helps PDAs and other Web connected devices decide whether to download or ignore a complex document.

Another overlooked part of a site – by people, not engines, is the page title box. In this instance, in your meta-tags type:

<HTML> (head) (title) (words describing the page contents and, if you like, your company name)

and these will appear on the page title. Throughout your site, you can further improve rankings by adding a comment section in the meta tags.

< - - (Additional explanation of what you do) then close with -)

Get registered – but not too soon
Eighty five percent of surfers will find you via search engines. So search engine companies are busy. Keep them happy by only submitting your site once you are sure it's ready. Having said that, if you are going to break your site down by page, never send in too many pages from the same URL at once; instead spread it out. The engine personnel are busy, but sharp. So don't attempt sending in misleading meta-tag descriptions.

In addition to viewing your coding, search engines may rank according to:

- Loading speed – the faster the download, the higher the ranking
- Spelling – poor spelling may suggest poor service
- Colour of text – worth dabbling with but consistency tends to work best (some engines have been known to give credit for vivid colours)

- Number of good links in addition to links to other sites – which should be invited to link back to you. Always ensure that every sub-page within your site links back to your home page
- Relevance to subject – if your site is just a façade for something other than its category listing you will plummet down the rankings
- Value added features like chat rooms, e-zines and searchable databases.

Watching the competition

There are two sides to a chain's link. Here's the other half of the story. If your competitor is ranked higher than you, try the search engine 'link': technique on that site. Perhaps some of those links would like to couple up with you. If you want to find as many competitors as possible, apart from the ones you already know, go to your favourite engine and look for an option to 'find sites like this'.

Looking at your competitors' meta-tags, do they feature something that you don't? If everything is just about equal, you could find the problem is that you simply misspelt a few meta-tag keywords.

Well that's about it – for now. To share cybermarketing tips with readers for future editions or catch up on the latest innovations, please visit www.makemesuccessful.com. You've learned a lot in just seven days – now take the next steps towards a successful cybermarketing future for you and your organisation. Good luck!

Gabay's Winning imperatives Of the Web
(The WOW steps)

1. Never forget: ultimately you are dealing with people, not computers.
2. People are social animals, so use the Web to unite communities throughout the global economy.
3. Build bridges between your organisation and all connecting to it using intra and extra networks.
4. News on the Web, good or bad, travels fast. Remain commercially aware and socially responsible.
5. No one will pay for anything on the Web until and unless you pay attention to them.
6. Cyber brands reflect what people need, not what you want – deliver and make their attainment rewarding.
7. It's no longer 'us and them', sales and marketing or IT and management: become a marketing communications *integrator*.
8. However far the Web reaches, land, sea or air, never lose sight that it's only as powerful as your original simple business objective.
9. Today's cyber technology is tomorrow's Morse code. If you can't enhance your cybermarketing your strategy is misled and tactics out-dated.
10. Without consistent cybermarketing, the average product life cycle of a website is just months – aim to live long and prosper!

e-mail: jj@theworks.co.uk